Call Me Little Theresa

St. Theresa of Lisieux

by
Susan Helen Wallace, FSP

Introduction by
Bishop Patrick V. Ahern, DD

Illustrations by
Nino Musio

Pauline
BOOKS & MEDIA
BOSTON

Library of Congress Cataloging-in-Publication Data

Wallace, Susan Helen, 1940-
    Call me little Theresa : St. Theresa of Lisieux / by Susan Helen Wallace ; introduction by Patrick V. Ahern ; illustrations by Nino Musio.
        p.   cm.
    Summary : A biography of the French woman who entered the Carmelite order at the age of fifteen, died of tuberculosis at twenty-four, and was canonized in 1925.
    Includes bibliographical references.
    ISBN 0-8198-1534-9
    1. Thérèse, de Lisieux, Saint, 1873-1897—Juvenile literature. 2. Christian saints—France—Biography—Juvenile literature. [1. Thérèse, de Lisieux, Saint, 1873-1897. 2. Saints.] I. Musio, Nino, ill. II. Title
BX4700.T5W35   1995
282'.092—dc20
[B]   95-12898
                                                                                CIP
                                                                                 AC

The quotations of St. Theresa have been taken from *Story of a Soul*, translated by John Clarke, O.C.D. Copyright © 1975, 1976 by Washington Province of Discalced Carmelites Friars, Inc., ICS Publications, 2131 Lincoln Road, N.E. Washington, D.C. 20002 U.S.A. Used with permission. St. Theresa's direct quotations are from this version of *Story of a Soul*.

"A Prayer to Obtain the Spirit of St. Theresa" by Bishop Patrick V. Ahern, DD, on p. 91 is used with permission.

The following prayers: "My Novena Rose Prayer," "Miraculous Prayer of St. Theresa" and "Novena Prayer for Vocations" on pp. 92-93 are used with permission of: Society of the Little Flower, 1313 Frontage Rd., Darien, IL 60559.

The following prayers: "Prayer to Learn the 'Little Way' of St. Theresa" and "Stay With us, Jesus" on pp. 93-94 are used with permission of: The Monastery of St. Joseph, Discalced Carmelites, Terre Haute, IN 47802.

Printed and published in the U.S.A. by Pauline Books & Media, 50 St. Paul's Avenue, Boston, MA 02130.

http://www.pauline.org

Pauline Books & Media is the publishing house of the Daughters of St. Paul, an international congregation of women religious serving the Church with the communications media.

2 3 4 5 6 7   04 03 02 01 00 99 98

For my parents,
Helen and Leo Wallace,
who, like the parents of Theresa Martin,
saw their children as gifts

"When the saints have closed the gates of heaven on me, they will sing:

'At last we have you,
Little gray mouse,
At last, we have you
And we won't let you go!'"

St. Theresa of the Child Jesus
"Her Last Conversations," p. 103

Contents

PRAYERS WE CAN SAY TO HONOR
ST. THERESA OF THE CHILD JESUS:

Introduction

St. Theresa of Lisieux lived during the last quarter of the nineteenth century, when the modern age was coming to birth. Ours is the age of science and technology. No one would call it the age of faith.

To show this age a confidence in his merciful love that no trial could ever shake, God raised up this amazing woman. The dimensions of her greatness are only now coming fully to light. Her faith was put under siege by the forces of skepticism all around her. With heroic courage she withstood the attack. In the much quoted phrase of Pope St. Pius X, she emerged from her struggle as "the greatest saint of modern times."

St. Theresa is the saint for everyone. Her autobiography, in fifty languages, has been read by countless millions in every corner of the world. She is especially the saint for young people, for she died at age twenty-four. As a teenager she bravely stood her ground against all the problems that threatened to block her maturing, and carved out her own future as one of the greatest contemplatives in history. A prodigy of holiness and intelligence, she offers to young people the model they so urgently need as they struggle with their deep and frightening crises. To negotiate the rapids of adolescence is no easy task. It is hard and demanding to find one's way to becoming the man or woman each of us is destined to be.

I am delighted that Sister Susan Helen Wallace has seen the need of introducing St. Theresa to young people. They need to know her story. They need to be ready for the great moment when they will take up her incomparable autobiography. They will encounter in it the amazing depth of her wisdom and strength. Both young women and young men need a heroine who will challenge them and love them. They need a heroine who will be a friend to support them and walk the long journey of life with them. Above all, young people need *hope,* and I have never known anyone to equal St. Theresa for inspiring hope. She is able to light up the darkest moments.

Sister Susan has given us a fine book, written in clear and simple prose. The illustrations by Nino Musio are convincing portraits of a saint who is real. This book will make a suitable gift for any child making First Holy Communion or Confirmation. It is indeed a handsome present on any occasion to someone who is young.

Bishop Patrick V. Ahern, DD

Theresa Is Born

January 2, 1873, was a cold and gray day in Alencon, France. There was excitement in the Martin home as the four girls waited anxiously for the new baby's arrival. Marie was the oldest, followed by Pauline, Leonie and Celine. Would they have a brother or a sister? Mama looked so frail. Four children had died in infancy. This baby would be her ninth. The girls prayed in their hearts that all would go well and continued to do their chores.

Papa Martin was his usual serene self. He was always there, so steady, so reliable. He was nervous, but didn't show it. Papa leaned over the bed and kissed his wife on the cheek. He whispered her name softly, almost like a prayer. "Zelie," he said, touching her head. Their eyes met and Zelie smiled. It wouldn't be long now.

***

Louis Martin had been born on August 22, 1823. He was good with his hands and hard-working. Louis took his faith seriously. When he was twenty, he even felt attracted to the life of a monk. He applied to join an order of monks. But Louis was told that he needed to learn Latin to be able to chant the Divine Office. "Go and finish your Latin studies," the prior advised. "Then come back and apply again." Louis prayed and asked for advice. He began to realize that a monk's life was not really for him. Instead, he became a watchmaker and ran a successful jewelry shop.

Azelie-Marie, known as Zelie, was a maker of the kind of lace for which Alencon had become famous. Zelie had thought about becoming a sister. But she realized that she wanted to be a wife and a mother. Louis and Zelie met and fell in love. They shared common interests and values. The couple married on July 12, 1858. The Catholic faith was as much a part of their lives as their love for each other. That same love reached out and embraced their children.

***

The ninth child of Zelie and Louis Martin was a girl. Their oldest, Marie, was chosen to be godmother. The family was radiant as the baby was baptized Marie Francoise Theresa. They decided to call her Theresa for short.

In all the excitement, Papa kept his worries to himself. The baby and Zelie were so fragile. Silently he prayed for the courage to do his best for them.

***

January and February passed slowly. By early March, the Martin girls were anxious for signs of spring. It wouldn't be much longer. Soon buds would be sprouting and leaves would return to the trees.

Louis and Zelie were worried about the baby. Theresa was small and pale. Her eyes glowed. Perhaps she had a fever. Zelie's health was poor as well. The doctor advised country air and a nurse for the baby. This meant the Martins would have to part with Theresa for a while. Zelie winced but agreed. Baby Theresa was sent to the home of Rose Taille about eight miles outside Alencon. Theresa had to remain there over a year, from the middle of March 1873 until April 2, 1874. When she was returned, Theresa and the family adjusted quickly. The Martins lifted her, hugged her, kissed her and played with her. It was wonderful having her back home.

Mama's Memories

Zelie watched Celine and Theresa, her two youngest, play blocks together. As the girls passed through the "block playing" stage, their mother was amazed at Celine's patience and Theresa's tantrums. Her youngest was very serious about everything she did, even playing blocks.

Although Theresa was three years younger than Celine, she tried to be the leader. Celine was simple and unsuspecting. She willingly let Theresa lead. Once in a while, the girls would argue. Usually, Celine would quickly give in. But there were tantrums too. Theresa would purse her lips and stamp her feet. To Mama's amazement, she occasionally rolled on the floor and cried so hard she nearly choked. But Mrs. Martin knew how to handle Theresa. Time passed, and the girls became constant companions.

"Celine and Theresa are always together," Mrs. Martin wrote to Pauline, who was at boarding school. "It would be impossible to find two sisters closer."

When Celine had to stop playing to have her school lessons at home, Theresa waited in the next room. She pulled up a chair and practiced threading beads or sewing. The needlework was difficult because the needle kept unthreading. Theresa's little fingers struggled to push the thread through the needle's eye. She did not succeed. She would sit there struggling until her oldest sister, Marie, would pass by and come to the rescue. Mama, busy about her chores, often did not realize Theresa's frustration until after it had been taken care of. It was so hard waiting for hours for Celine, Theresa thought. Why couldn't she have lessons too?

Marie introduced her two youngest sisters to the habit of making acts of love for Jesus throughout the day. Marie had been taught at the Visitation convent school to carry a little chain of movable beads. Every time she prayed an act of love, a bead would be pushed up on the chain. Celine and Theresa were very impressed with this practice. Each made a chain, and they put them in the pockets of their dresses. Marie helped the girls see the many ways they could make an act of love of God throughout the day. The girls would say a prayer, obey right away, go out of their way to be thoughtful, clean up their toys. A quiet competition grew between them. Often, before supper, they would meet at their hiding place under the bushes in the garden. There the two little girls would carefully count the number of beads to see who had "won" that day, who had made the most acts of love for Jesus. Mama was happy with them. They decided that Jesus must be happy with them, too.

***

March 29, 1875 was a wonderful day for a train ride. Theresa felt proud and excited. Just she and Mama were going to Le Mans to visit Sister Marie Dosithee, Mama's older sister.

The convent of the Order of the Visitation grew bigger and bigger as Theresa approached it. Suddenly, for no obvious reason, tears spilled down her cheeks and wouldn't stop. Her aunt bent over and kissed her little tear-stained niece, whom she was meeting for the first time. They had a nice visit.

As Mrs. Martin and Theresa were about to leave, Sister Marie gave Theresa a small basket of candies and a white toy mouse. The little girl's eyes glowed. She thanked her aunt and clung tightly to the basket handle with one hand and her mother's hand with the other. Going down the convent steps, Theresa was so excited, swinging her little basket. Suddenly she realized that most of the candy had spilled along the way. She had wanted to bring the treats home for Celine. Now what could she do? Could she go back? She sobbed softly, as she skipped along, trying to keep up with Mama. Mrs. Martin did not seem to notice. The little girl began to cry loudly. But Mama only hurried her gently along. Perhaps they would miss the train, or Mama may have had something on her mind. Theresa couldn't understand why Mama did not console her.

When Theresa Said "No"

The sound of the key in the front door lock meant one thing to Theresa: Papa was home. Wherever she was in the big house, Theresa managed to hear the sound and would come running. "Papa, Papa," she would call. She would hug and kiss her father and then sit firmly on his shoe. Papa let her ride his foot, pony-fashion, into the sitting room. The little girl squealed with delight. Papa was so much fun.

"Why do you spoil her like that?" Mama would chide quietly. Papa would throw up his hands good-naturedly and ask, "What do you expect? She is my little queen."

Theresa was the youngest child and she liked being the little queen.

One afternoon, she was having a wonderful time by herself in the garden. She was swinging, higher and higher. Papa walked down the path. "Come and kiss me, little queen," he called kindly.

"Come and get the kiss yourself!" Theresa said as she continued to swing. The sensitive man was hurt. He refused and walked softly away. One of her sisters had watched the whole thing. Marie stopped Theresa's swing. She chided Theresa for the way she had treated Papa. "How naughty of you to act like that," Marie said, crossing her arms and frowning.

The little girl was instantly sorry. She hung her head and began to cry so loudly that her voice carried into every room of the Martins' large house.

***

Another day, Theresa and Celine were having fun outside. Their next oldest sister, Leonie, came to them. She carried a basket filled with pretty material. Her doll was perched on top. Leonie was feeling much too grown up for dolls. She smiled and held out the basket. "Choose," she said. Celine selected a small ball of yarn she could use for making something nice. Theresa thought for a moment and said, "I choose all of it," and she took the basket right out of Leonie's hands. No one minded, not even Celine, who had many toys and other nice things. Theresa never forgot this incident. It was the way she wanted to love and serve Jesus. As a nun, she would one day write, "My God, I choose all. I don't want to be a saint *by halves*, I'm not afraid to suffer for you. I fear only one thing: to keep my *own will*; so take it, for *'I choose all'* that you will!"

Mama Goes Home

Papa's forehead was wrinkled. The Martin girls had learned to read his face as accurately as they could read a book. They knew Papa was worried about their mother's health. Eventually, Zelie became so ill that she could no longer move about without extreme pain. The doctor had told her that her cancer was fatal and she did not have long to live. She had been shaken by the hard news at first, but then she had forced herself to pray. Louis Martin sent her with her two oldest daughters to Lourdes. All during the long week they were away, Mr. Martin waited for the telegram announcing the miraculous cure of his wife. No telegram came, but when Zelie returned and stepped off the train in Alencon, she looked peaceful. She had received from the Virgin of Lourdes the strength and serenity she would need for the journey to her eternal home.

At first Zelie must have asked the Lord for a little more time to see her children grow up and get settled. Theresa was only four. But the pain increased daily, and strength was wrung out of Zelie by the illness. Her growing awareness of her suffering as a gift of love to Jesus for her family made her resigned. And Louis was such a loving father, she thought to herself. He had enough love for his children to make up for both of them. The Lord and his Mother would be with him.

August 1877 was hot and humid in Alencon. The Martins spent hours at their mother's bedside. They prayed with her, took care of her needs, cheered her, cried with her. They decorated her room with flowers. Little Theresa was there sometimes too. She was very quiet, as quiet as the little toy mouse her nun-aunt in Le Mans had given her. During their mother's final days, Theresa and Celine were packed off each morning to the home of a cousin who lived close by. The little girls talked about Mama and worried about her. They felt like homeless children, lost in the shuffle and confusion.

All five Martin children gathered with Papa around their mother's bed when the priest arrived. He anointed Mrs. Martin. All the while, Louis Martin sobbed. Little Theresa knelt, frozen to the spot. She wanted to hug Papa, but she stayed near her sisters instead. Zelie died on August 28, 1877. Papa picked up Theresa and held her over the casket. He told her to kiss her Mama for the last time. Theresa's lips touched her mother's cold forehead.

Then Papa set her down. Zelie's funeral, in the parish church of Notre Dame, took place the next day. The loss was so great that Papa and the girls could only share their grief in silence. They tried to help one another, to lighten the load, but the emptiness left each of them alone with their sadness.

The family buried Mrs. Martin and returned home. They became aware of the youngest member of the family, who had spent the least number of years with Zelie. Sometimes Theresa seemed her age; at other times she seemed older. Today she was four, a child who had lost her mother. Her eyes were red from crying. She looked at her sisters and made her own choice. She asked Pauline if she would become her second mother. Pauline hugged Theresa and accepted.

Farewell to Alencon

Aunt and Uncle Guerin were loving relatives. Uncle Guerin was Zelie's brother. Zelie knew the Guerins would help Louis raise the girls. The couple owned a profitable pharmacy in Lisieux. To be near them, Mr. Martin decided to move there.

The big house in Alencon swelled with memories and echoes of Mrs. Martin. The family loved Alencon. Louis had sound business ties there. But he wanted his girls to benefit from the loving guidance of their Aunt Celine and Uncle Isidore. The couple was called Aunt and Uncle Guerin. They loved their nieces as if they were their own daughters. Uncle Guerin became their deputy guardian and brought the family to their new home.

While the Guerins helped the Martin family move in, Papa stayed behind to conclude business transactions in Alencon. The family moved in on November 15, 1877. Marie took over the management of the house. Pauline took care of the upbringing of her three younger sisters. Leonie, Celine and Theresa busily explored their new surroundings.

Saying good-bye to Alencon had been hard for the older girls, but once they were in Lisieux, they became involved in day-to-day living. Theresa and Celine had no difficulty moving to a new place. They thought it was exciting. They had been greeted warmly by Aunt and Uncle Guerin's children, nine-year-old Jeanne and seven-year-old Marie. Theresa loved her cousins. Celine, Jeanne, Marie and Theresa enjoyed playing games and having fun.

The house at Lisieux had a name. In French it was called *Les Buissonnets,* which means the little bushes.

Papa the King

Papa finished his work in Alencon and came to Lisieux. His daughters were thrilled. They took him through the entire house and disclosed its secrets to him. Theresa knew what he would like best: the *belvedere.* This was a small room on the top floor. Mr. Martin *did* like it. He adopted it for his study. Papa would also enjoy the backyard garden, which would be alive with flowers and plants during spring and summer.

Theresa often thought of her mother. But in the new house, she began to feel happy again. She became more talkative and playful. Papa encouraged this. Often he was hard at work at his desk in the study. In warm weather, he would be reading in the garden. But he was always available for his family. Theresa had no doubt about this. When Papa was upstairs, she would climb the steps to chat a while. Often she approached her king, took his hand, and pulled him good-naturedly. Sometimes she invited him to come to the garden to see her newest invention. Other times she picked flowers and arranged them on a flat rock in the wall surrounding the back-

yard. She had made the little nook into a shrine. Theresa would bring Papa there. The two would stand in front of the shrine and Mr. Martin would make a big fuss about its beauty.

Then Theresa invited Papa to have homemade refreshments. She made pretend tea out of bark and seeds she found on the ground. Theresa served Papa graciously. He acted as if he were really drinking her special brew. Then he would ask out of the side of his mouth softly, "Should I throw it out now?" Sometimes Theresa would say yes, but usually she would ask him to save it. She could play the game several more times that day.

Every afternoon Papa took Theresa for a walk to a different church. Together father and daughter made a visit to Jesus in the Blessed Sacrament. One day Papa took his little queen to the chapel of the cloistered Carmelite nuns. They prayed and then Mr. Martin showed Theresa the grill that separated the nuns from them. Theresa never even imagined that nine years later she would be in that very convent on the other side of the grill.

Together as Family

Papa was strict about his family's recreation. The Martins did not take part in the active social life of Lisieux with its constant events and parties. But they were happy just the same. Papa loved the nearby park as much as the girls did. They went there often for walks, had picnic lunches and enjoyed conversations. While Papa flung his fishing pole line into the water, his daughters did needlework or painted and sketched. Pauline painted on parchment and ivory. Celine began to take drawing and painting lessons.

Frequently family evening time began with Theresa lighting the oil lamp and calling to Papa to come down from his study. It was time for him to play a game of checkers with the opponent of the evening. Often times Marie was his opponent because she was the best player, almost as good as Papa. The other girls did their hobbies

and watched. Then the time came for Theresa's older sisters to read aloud. Sometimes they would read about the spiritual lessons that could be learned from the Church's liturgy. Other evenings, the reading was from a variety of interesting and enriching books. Theresa was a good listener. She loved to hear stories about the saints, too.

While the older girls read *La Croix*, the Catholic daily newspaper, to keep up on world and local events, Theresa busied herself with her pets and toys. She had a dog named Tom, rabbits, doves and goldfish. She had interesting toys, too. There was a miniature stove, doll house-size pots and pans, a wheelbarrow, a top, a trumpet, a jump rope and a toy piano. She was not interested in dolls, but chose to play with animals or toys instead.

Sunday: God's Feast Day

Papa kept Sundays for the Lord. Sunday was what Theresa called "God's feast day." They were feast days for her, too. Pauline let her sleep a little later because Sunday was a day of rest. While she was still in bed, Pauline would bring her a cup of chocolate to drink. It was so exciting. Then Pauline got her up. She dressed Theresa in one of her Sunday outfits. Soon Marie was at the bedroom door. She had a hair brush and began to brush Theresa's blonde curls. Sometimes this hurt and Theresa would pout when Marie accidentally pulled her hair. But in the end, the little girl was glad about it because she was ready to go with her king to church.

Every Sunday Papa would take Theresa's hand and kiss it. Then, hand in hand, father and youngest daughter would walk to church accompanied by Marie, Pauline, Leonie and Celine. People smiled because all during Mass the child clung to Papa's hand. When she was a nun, Theresa wrote about going to Mass with Papa and the family: "Everyone seemed to think it so wonderful to see such a handsome old man with such a little daughter."

Theresa tried hard to pay attention during the sermon. She could not understand too much, the way Papa did. He often had tears in his eyes, which he wiped quickly away. But Theresa did understand one sermon. It was about the sufferings of Jesus on the cross. After that, Theresa felt that she understood all the rest of the sermons she was to hear. When the preacher mentioned her patron, St. Teresa of Avila, Papa would lean over and whisper for her to listen carefully. Theresa wanted to. She was proud of her patron saint.

The rest of Sunday was filled with walks and family dinner. Then the Martins returned to church in late afternoon for prayer. After supper the girls took turns visiting the Guerins. When it was Theresa's turn, Papa would arrive to take her home promptly at 8 PM. They would walk together and study the stars. One cluster seemed to form the letter "T." "Papa, look," she said. "My name is written in heaven."

Around this time, Theresa made her first confession to Father Ducellier, who was a priest at Saint-Pierre Cathedral. He also preached the sermon on the sufferings of Jesus that Theresa talked often about.

Summertime

Even when Theresa was too little to go to school with Leonie and Celine, she received lessons at home. Marie gave her writing lessons and Pauline taught the rest. Theresa liked catechism and sacred history the best. Her sisters helped her apply herself to her schoolwork, and Papa praised her for her effort and good grades. Summertime brought a welcome change of pace. During vacation, Theresa loved to go fishing with Papa. She would take out her own small pole and fish alongside her father. But soon the little girl would lose interest. She would sit quietly on the grass and look at the flowers, the clouds, the water, the trees, the birds. And she would pray. She thought about God and all the beautiful gifts of nature he had created.

One time, before going home, Theresa opened her little picnic basket and pulled out the treat prepared by Pauline. "Papa, look," Theresa said with a frown. The jelly that had been bright and delicious-looking a few hours before was now dull. The fresh, homemade bread slices were broken and crumpled. How fast things change in this life, Theresa thought.

Another time, Theresa was watching the clouds as Papa fished. Suddenly they began to change form and grow dark. As lightning flashed and drops of rain began to fall, Papa packed up. They had to cross several fields of tall grass before arriving home so Papa hoisted Theresa on his back. Then he picked up his gear and walked quickly through the sparkling fields. There was nothing to be afraid of, the child thought as she hung on tightly. When she was with Papa, she was safe.

***

Aunt Guerin rented a summer villa and the Martins were invited to spend a few weeks near the sea. Theresa's first visit was on August 8, 1878. She was five years old. She described later in her writings the beauty of the sea and the roaring of the waves. Papa and Theresa walked along the shore. Theresa often darted ahead of her father and let the water splash her feet and ankles. A young couple came up to Mr. Martin and said that Theresa was a pretty little girl. They asked if the child was his daughter. Mr. Martin said yes, and motioned to the couple not to make too much fuss about it. But Theresa had heard and she remembered the care her family took not to let her become spoiled.

Theresa gazed out at the boats sailing on the sea. She imagined herself as a little sailboat moving steadily toward Jesus.

Papa and Theresa
—the "Givers"

Papa was from the part of France called Normandy. The Normans, he said, were known to be good business-people. Mr. Martin realized that he, too, had a good business sense. He was successful and had enough money to take good care of his family. He also believed that a Christian had an obligation not only to run his business honestly, but to share with the poor. Papa had a sensitive heart for the suffering and the poor. He wanted to help relieve their burdens, but was prudent in the way he did this. He was always a teacher, realizing that his children's eyes followed him wherever he went. He informally established Monday afternoons as open house for needy people to come to his home to ask for help. Some were given food or money, or both. He also helped to educate and sponsor other people who needed a good recommendation and a steady income. Mr. Martin would take a personal interest in the people he helped. He would back them up, and would inquire about their needs. He was there for them when they wanted the advice of a friend.

During their walks together, Papa would often have Theresa bring alms (food and money) to give to the poor.

"On one occasion," Theresa wrote later, "we met a poor man who was dragging himself along painfully on crutches. I went up to give him a coin. He looked at me with a sad smile and refused my offering since he felt he wasn't poor enough to accept alms. I cannot express the feeling that went through my heart. I wanted to console this man and instead I had given him pain or so I thought. The poor invalid undoubtedly guessed at what was passing through my mind, for I saw him turn around and smile at me.

"Papa had just bought me a little cake, and I had an intense desire to give it to the man, but I didn't dare. However, I really wanted to give him something he couldn't refuse, so great was the sympathy I felt toward him. I remembered having heard that on our First Communion day we can obtain whatever we ask for, and this thought greatly consoled me. Although I was only six years old at this time, I said: 'I'll pray for this poor man the day of my First Communion.' I kept my promise five years later, and I hope God answered the prayer he inspired me to direct to him in favor of one of his suffering members."

The Mysterious Vision

One afternoon, Papa was away and was not expected back until late. Theresa's sisters were busy doing their usual tasks. Theresa was by herself near a window that overlooked the garden. She was six or seven years old, she recalled when talking about the incident many years later. The sun was bright at that time of day (around 2 or 3 PM). Theresa gazed out the window. The garden was so beautiful. She felt good inside. Slowly a figure appeared near the wash house. He was the size and height of Papa, but he was older and bent. A thick veil hid his face. He walked slowly, carefully through the garden. Theresa felt overwhelmed with fear and cried, "Papa, Papa." The man didn't seem to hear the frightened child. He kept walking toward the clump of fir trees that divided the garden walk. Theresa thought that he would go beyond the trees and reappear again, but he was gone.

The whole experience took only a minute, but the little girl was badly shaken. Marie and Pauline had heard the cry and came rushing into the room. Trying to be calm, Marie asked gently, "Theresa, why are you calling Papa? You know he is in Alencon today." Theresa's story gushed out. Her sisters tried to convince her that the maid had covered her head to play a joke on Theresa. Victoire, the maid, was questioned. She insisted that she had not left the kitchen. Theresa knew it was not Victoire. It was Papa, old and bent and suffering. They searched every bit of the backyard to find the man, but he had vanished.

What did the vision mean? Someday Theresa would realize that the mysterious vision meant her father would have a painful cross—strokes, partial paralysis and mental difficulties—for three years before his death. And Papa's pain would be suffered by all his daughters. Theresa remembered the vision often. She couldn't stand to think that her king would bear a heavy cross.

"Jesus," Theresa whispered in her heart, "please take care of my king."

***

One day Mr. Martin was on the top rung of the ladder, fixing something on the house. Theresa was right with him, under the ladder, watching patiently. "Move away, my little queen," Papa called down. "If I fall, I might hurt you." Theresa remembered this little incident even when she was grown up. "I don't want to move away," she said to herself. "I want to stay right here with Papa. If he is going to fall, I will fall too. This way I will not have the pain of seeing him die."

Theresa the Student

Theresa took her studies seriously. She did not try to take advantage of her tutors, Pauline and Marie. Theresa did her homework assignments and studied hard. She was a high achiever and liked to learn, but she had to work for her good grades. Now she was going to attend a nearby boarding school run by the Benedictine nuns. She was eight and a half years old and wondered what it would be like. She and Celine would be day students because the school was near enough for them to return home each evening.

Until that time, Theresa had been surrounded by her family and cousins. She knew the families in her neighborhood and they knew her. In fact, even the next door neighbor's pet parrot had picked up her name from conversations he heard over picnics in the Martins' backyard. "Theresa, Theresa," the parrot would call over and over. That made Theresa laugh. But outside her small, peaceful world, Theresa felt afraid and shy.

This was only normal. And she could have adjusted to boarding school without a problem if it hadn't been for one student who picked on her. Theresa was to spend five years at the school; she later called them "the saddest in her life." Because Theresa's sisters had tutored her at home, she found herself in an advanced class at the abbey. One girl, about fourteen years old, found learning difficult. Theresa was younger and smaller, but she learned much more quickly. The better Theresa's grades, the more the other girl made fun of her.

Theresa felt like crying almost every day. She knew that the girl made the others stay away from her and ignore her. Theresa was very hurt. She asked Jesus to help her understand and love the girl who was causing her so much trouble. Meanwhile, she never complained to anyone about the way she was being treated. When she was with her family in the evenings, she would climb up on Papa's lap and listen to his wonderful stories. Her sisters would hug her and help her with her schoolwork. Her loving family made

up for the way she was being treated at school.

Theresa and Celine grew even closer. Theresa loved her cousins, Jeanne and Marie, too. She and Marie were great playmates. Theresa told the story as a grownup about an evening when she and Celine were walking home from the abbey with Jeanne and Marie. Theresa decided to pretend she couldn't see. She asked Marie to lead her home. Marie steered her cousin down the sidewalk. Then she decided that it would be even more fun if she closed her eyes too. So two blind little girls bumped into crates and spilled merchandise in front of a store. The angry owner came out and chased the children—who could suddenly see well enough to run as fast as necessary to get away.

In describing Celine, Theresa said that when they were little, Celine had been very gentle and well-behaved. Theresa had been naughty and hard to handle. Later, Celine was full of mischief and Theresa was quiet and sensitive. The two sisters grew closer and closer. They bought gifts for each other. Papa paid the bills for their small but important treasures. Theresa was as happy for Celine on her First Communion day as if it were her own. Theresa was caught off guard when her second mother, Pauline, told her gently that she was going to leave the family to become a nun. Pauline was so happy about going to Carmel. Theresa felt the way she did when Mama had died. What was Carmel? she wondered. How could Pauline leave her?

Papa, Marie, Leonie and Celine were as loving as ever. But the house seemed empty without Pauline. Pauline had joined a cloistered group of sisters called the Carmelites. Papa had taken Theresa to pray in their chapel one afternoon when she was a little girl. Now Pauline, her dear second mother, would be there, behind the big wall. It was October 2, 1882. Theresa was nine. She and her cousin Marie met Mother Gonzague. Theresa asked Mother if she could become a Carmelite too. Mother Gonzague was kind and hopeful. She encouraged Theresa to prepare herself by living a good Christian life. Then, when she was old enough, she could return. Theresa thought about this wonderful life. She began to see that it was *beautiful* not just because Pauline had chosen it, but because the Carmelite nun makes Jesus the great love of her life.

Theresa's Mysterious Illness

At the end of 1882 Theresa began to have very bad headaches. Pauline had left home to join nuns who were cloistered. To a child, it was as if Pauline were dead. She was gone from Theresa's life. Marie had become an even more loving big sister and godmother. But the sensitive heart of Theresa burst because she had lost two mothers in her first ten years of life. She was not yet aware that the sorrows, sufferings and disappointments of life are the way a Christian can share in the cross of Jesus. Despite her headaches, Theresa went to school and did her homework as usual.

During Easter time, 1883, Papa took Marie and Leonie to Paris. The two youngest girls stayed with Aunt and Uncle Guerin. One evening her uncle took Theresa for a walk. He spoke gently to her about her mother and his many treasured memories of her. Her uncle suggested that Theresa should let herself have a wonderful Easter vacation. It would do her good to have fun, he said. Theresa was impressed by the loving concern for her. Uncle and Aunt Guerin were like second parents. That evening she was supposed to go with them to a Catholic Circle meeting. Instead she became sick, shaking, as if with a fever. Her aunt covered her with blankets and surrounded her with hot water bottles. But the shaking continued throughout the night. When the rest of the Martins returned home from Paris, Theresa was very ill. Papa and Marie cared for her. Theresa could not be taken back home, so Marie moved in with the Guerins to take care of her little sister.

On the day that Pauline was to receive the habit of a Carmelite nun, Theresa was well enough to be taken to the convent. She was permitted to see Pauline, sit on her lap, hug and kiss her. Then she was taken back to her own home while Papa walked Pauline, the radiant bride of Jesus, down the aisle of the chapel. Pauline was Papa's first gift to Jesus. The Lord would ask him to offer four more—his entire earthly treasure. Papa was quiet and prayerful throughout the ceremony. Tears lit his eyes as he pictured the face of his wife Zelie. If only she could be here, he thought. But then, of course, she was, even though he could not see her with his human eyes.

On April 7, 1883, the frightening illness swept over the child again. Theresa seemed to be delirious, babbling phrases that did not connect or

make sense. It was as if the devil, or a hundred devils, were loose in her room. Everything became distorted. Some simple objects would catch her eye, like nails sticking out in the wood. Then, as the terrified girl watched, the nails would twist and turn into large, crawling spiders. Her father stood silently by her bed and suffered in his heart all that his little queen felt. As Theresa fixed her eyes on Papa's hat, it changed its form and became grotesque. Theresa screamed and Papa left the room sobbing.

The family prayed and kept their vigil beside Theresa's bed. They begged Mary, the Mother of God, for a cure. Papa gave Marie money to send to Paris to have a novena of Masses celebrated at Our Lady of Victories. "A miracle was necessary," Theresa said many years later, "and Our Lady of Victories worked it." During the novena, Marie entered Theresa's room. Theresa was calling "Mama, Mama" in low tones, as she often did. Marie knelt in tears before the family statue of Our Lady. She asked our Heavenly Mother to cure her suffering little sister, to release her from the powers of darkness. Suddenly, our Lady appeared to Theresa. The only word to describe her was *beautiful.* The Virgin's smile held Theresa spellbound. She felt riveted to the Mother of God. Suddenly, her pain and fear vanished. Theresa felt peaceful, as if she had never had the illness at all. It was gone forever. Two soft tears formed on the child's eyelids and slid down her face.

Theresa was cured.

The Abbey Retreat

The retreat that prepared the girls for First Communion lasted four days. The girls followed a schedule similar to a convent schedule. They got up early, washed and dressed, then had a balance of spiritual events mingled with meals. These days had a special wonder about them. Even though Theresa was separated from her family, they were in her thoughts and prayers. They came for a short daily visit, though, and brought candy and pastries for her to share with her friends.

Theresa acted responsibly during the retreat, the way her family had trained her. But she did arrive at a startling realization. She was expected to get up quietly and quickly, wash and dress herself, and comb her own hair. The last part was difficult. Her curls were thick and challenging. Marie combed her hair every morning. Now, suddenly, she wasn't there. Theresa picked up her comb and went quietly to the teacher in charge of the dormitory. "My sister Marie usually combs my hair," Theresa said shyly. "Would you do it please?" "A big girl like you?" the teacher asked the eleven-year-old with a playful smile. But she took the comb good-naturedly, and did her work. She pulled the curls more

than Marie did, but Theresa didn't dare make a sound. She remembered how she cried almost every day when gentle Marie pulled her hair.

It was so exciting to realize that Pauline was making her retreat at Carmel in preparation for her first vows. Theresa would be receiving her First Communion the same day that Pauline would pronounce her vows.

Theresa began to realize that she felt just as close to Pauline as if she were still at home. How she treasured Pauline's weekly letter sent just to her. Theresa received a large crucifix from Leonie. During the retreat, she tucked it in her belt and wore it the way the missionaries did. In free moments, Theresa would go behind her bed and imagine she was in a little hut like a monk. There behind the hanging bed curtain she would think about God and holy things. This kind of thinking is a form of prayer called mental prayer or meditation.

As the day for Theresa to receive her First Holy Communion grew closer, she read many books. Some were books of lives of saints. Others were histories and stories of chivalry. They were all wholesome books and she loved to draw out lessons from what she read. She wanted to learn. Her reading helped her schoolwork, and Theresa thanked God for her family's interest in her. They guided what she read and helped her make wise choices.

One morning, during the retreat, Theresa spied Celine approaching the school. She had made a special trip to bring her sister a holy picture of Jesus. Theresa was thrilled. She had also received a holy picture from Pauline. Theresa treasured her gifts and showed them to everyone. Father Pichon, the Carmelite, sent her a letter for her First Communion day. Theresa could not find words to explain her joy. Someday, she hoped, he would be her spiritual director at Carmel.

Theresa and Jesus—
Jesus and Theresa

To prepare her soul for Jesus, Theresa received the sacrament of Reconciliation. The evening before First Communion she asked each member of her family pardon for whatever she had done to offend them. Even though Pauline couldn't be there, Theresa felt her presence. And she believed that Mama was there, too.

The next day Marie helped Theresa put on the white dress she had bought for her little sister. She adjusted the veil to fit securely on Theresa's head of ringlet curls. Theresa felt so grown up, like a bride. She took part in the Eucharistic Celebration, listening to the Word and singing the hymns with meaning. This special celebration made her heart burst with joy. It was Jesus coming to her. He looked like a little wafer, a piece of bread, but the host was Jesus. Theresa believed that. She had waited patiently while Papa and her older sisters had received Holy Communion. At last, she could join them.

After she was a nun, Theresa described her First Communion in her *Story of a Soul*. The great experience was so clear in her mind that it seemed to have happened that morning instead of when she was eleven. When the Eucharist was placed on her tongue, Theresa felt warmth wrapping around her like a blanket. It was the same gentle presence she had become aware of when she was alone on the hillside talking and listening to Jesus in her heart. She remembered how beautiful it had been, keeping company with Jesus while Papa fished. Now that whole feeling was magnified as Theresa knelt, adoring her Lord in her heart. It was as if Jesus took over her heart. Their two hearts were blended into one, and the beat producing the life of that heart was Jesus' grace in her soul.

From now on Theresa would still be Theresa, because Jesus loved her as Theresa. But he would fill her with himself. And he would lead his child along the road of total trust, the way children love and follow their parents with trust. It was all too wonderful. Theresa prayed for her family, her relatives, her friends and all those she promised to remember in prayer. She prayed especially for the stranger who had refused her coin when she was six years old.

After the ceremony, tears rolled down Theresa's cheeks. The children kept glancing at her, not knowing what to do. Should they ask her what was wrong? Console her? Why was she crying? They decided it must be because her mother was dead. Imagine how Theresa must miss her—especially today. They also realized that Pauline, the Carmelite whom Theresa loved so much, could not be there. Of course, she was crying. They wished they could make her feel better. But they never could have imagined that Theresa's tears were tears of joy. "They could not understand," Theresa wrote as a nun, "that all the joy of heaven having entered my heart, this exiled heart was unable to bear it without shedding tears."

The Day Wasn't Over

In the afternoon Theresa and the other first communicants made the Act of Consecration to Mary. Theresa was chosen to read the prayer as her companions listened and shared the thoughts in their hearts. Theresa read the words carefully. She meant them. Mary was truly her Mother in a special way. She had lost her earthly Mama when she was so young.

Theresa enjoyed the celebration at home, too. Her family and relatives showed their affection and their love. She unwrapped each gift carefully and treasured it because of her love for the "giver." And wasn't that just the way it was with Jesus? He had come to her that morning in the Eucharist. And the very word *Eucharist* means gift.

Theresa was so happy to be alone later in the day with Papa, Marie, Leonie and Celine. Papa, her king, gave Theresa a wristwatch. Then he and his little queen walked to the Carmelite convent. They visited Pauline. It had been a wonderful day for her, too. Pauline had pronounced her vows as a nun. Theresa could see her through the grill. She still wore her crown of roses. How beautiful she was.

The Spirit's Special Gift

After Theresa's First Communion on May 8, 1884, she waited anxiously for the opportunity to receive the Lord again. That great moment came on Ascension Thursday. (Receiving daily Communion was not Church practice until 1910, when Pope St. Pius X encouraged this.) Theresa wished with all her heart to receive Jesus often.

Now she had her Confirmation to look forward to as well. There would be a short retreat, followed by the reception of the Sacrament. Bishop Hugonin confirmed Theresa on June 14, 1884. Leonie was her sponsor. The two sisters then received Communion. When writing about her Confirmation day, Theresa said this: "On that day I received the strength to suffer, for soon afterward the martyrdom of my soul was about to begin." Those words became more clear as Theresa went on a daily journey with Jesus, trying to please him.

Life continued as usual at the boarding school. The students were different from the group that had prepared to receive the sacraments. These girls did not even try to obey the rules or apply themselves to their schoolwork. That wasn't right. Theresa found it hard to find friends who wanted to have fun during recreation times and who were serious students too. Attending school at the abbey was bearable only because Theresa's best friend, her sister, Celine, went there too. Theresa did start a few initiatives, though, for all her shyness. She lovingly collected the dead birds on the abbey grounds and made a bird cemetery. A few other students helped her care for it.

Theresa also found the courage to use her imaginative gift of storytelling. During daily recess times, she would invent a novel and keep it going with a new contribution each day. She also applied herself even harder to her studies, especially religion. Father Domin, her teacher, called her his "little doctor." He meant a doctor of theology, someone who is very serious and very educated in the faith. Celine completed her schooling at the abbey. Theresa asked not to continue on. She left in the middle of the 1885-86 school term. She continued her schooling with private lessons in the home of Madame Papineau.

***

Theresa was asked by Jesus to share in his cross in a special way. He wanted her to give up still another person she loved. Wasn't Mama enough? Wasn't Pauline enough? Still another? Theresa's dear Marie followed her call to Carmel on October 15, 1886, the feast of the great Carmelite, St. Teresa of Avila. On October 7, a week before, Leonie had joined the Poor Clares but later left.

On May 31, 1887, Theresa became a member of the Children of Mary. She drew close in loving prayer to her Heavenly Mother. Papa, Celine and Theresa missed the family members who had left home to follow their calling.

But Theresa began to feel very grown up. After all, she was the youngest, the little queen. Yet even little queens become grownup queens.

Papa's Little Queen Grows Up!

Theresa noticed that the family home seemed bigger and quieter. It was lonelier now. The youngest child felt restless. Celine kept their bedroom tidied up and employees did the housework. Theresa read and played with her pets. She studied her lessons and did her homework. Best of all, she shared conversations and walks with Papa. But something was missing. She became overly sensitive and cried frequently. Then she would cry because she had cried. She was becoming frustrated with herself.

Behind this frustration was Theresa's desire to grow up instantly so that she could enter Carmel. She decided that God would have to work a miracle if his fourteen-year-old child was ever to grow up. Christmas Eve, 1886, came. The Martins attended midnight Mass. The Christ Child, born each Christmas Eve in the hearts of his people, filled Theresa's soul with joy, with grace. It was his gift to his child, from a God who had become a child. That night Theresa felt she had been given the grace to leave her childish ways behind and to grow up. From that time on, her touchiness and "cry sessions" disappeared. Jesus had taken them away so that Theresa would be free to love him totally.

The family arrived home from midnight Mass. As children, Theresa and Celine always ran to the corner of the living room near the chimney and found their shoes stuffed with gifts. It was one of the treasured customs of Christmas that children leave behind when they are grown up. Celine wanted Theresa to enjoy this custom one last time, so her shoes were waiting, full of surprises. Papa was tired. It was late and he lost his customary peaceful manner. He said with irritation, "Well, fortunately, this will be the last year." Celine tried to console Theresa, but that was not necessary. The tears, as usual, rushed to her eyes. Then she caught hold of herself and refused to give in to hurt feelings. She picked up the shoes and brought them to Papa, the way she had always done. She opened her gifts one at a time. In an instant the tone changed from annoyance to joy. Theresa's greatest gift was to realize that Jesus had accepted her effort and good will. She realized that all she had to do was trust that he would make her holy.

As the months of 1887 passed, Theresa recognized within her a fruit of Jesus' love in her heart. He helped her see how much her prayers and sacrifices were needed to save people who were far from God. Jesus wanted Theresa's love and generosity to make up for those who offended God. The teenager studied a picture of Jesus on the cross. She realized how much he loved all people—those who returned his love and those who rejected him. She became aware of his words, spoken in terrible pain, from the cross: "I thirst." Theresa wanted to share that thirst. She wanted to bring her Jesus a drink of cool water. She wanted to make him happy as she had made Papa happy. She was Papa's little queen. She would be Jesus' little spouse. Theresa began to thirst for the souls of great sinners. She asked Jesus to show her how to pray and sacrifice

so that sinners would repent of their evil deeds and be saved.

She heard talk about the trial of a man accused of murder. His name was Henri Pranzini. The Pranzini trial opened on July 9, 1887. It ended on July 13. Pranzini was found guilty and sentenced to death. His execution was scheduled for August 31. During that time, Theresa prayed and sacrificed for her first "spiritual child." The execution date drew closer. Pranzini refused to see a priest. He showed no external signs of sorrow for what he had done. Theresa could not stand the thought that because he was not sorry, he would lose his soul forever in hell. She confided her secret to Celine. They had a Mass offered for the unfortunate man. They asked the Lord in prayer to give Pranzini the grace of repentance through the merits of the saints of the whole Church—of every saint who ever lived or would live. Then Theresa begged Jesus for a sign that Pranzini had repented.

The day after the execution, Theresa opened the newspaper. It reported that the condemned man had not gone to confession. He went up to the scaffold and put his head on the block. Suddenly he turned, reached out and took the crucifix from the priest standing there. He kissed it three times just before he was killed. As Theresa read the account, she wept. She had received the sign of Pranzini's sorrow. She tried to hide so that she would not have to explain her tears. This episode impressed her so deeply that her trust in Jesus' mercy could never be shaken.

Theresa's
Call to Carmel

Theresa was fourteen and a half when she became deeply aware of her calling to Carmel. It was true that she missed Pauline and Marie, but Theresa felt attracted to the life of a Carmelite nun because she wanted to belong to Jesus. Who was Jesus for Theresa? He was the Teacher, the Healer, the Savior of each person in the entire world. Yet he was so often unnoticed by that very world. Theresa felt a magnet-like attraction to living a deeply spiritual life with Jesus at the center. He would be the senior partner, the loving Lord who would guide her in the ways he wanted her to go. Theresa was encouraged by Celine. The two were even closer than they had been as children. They were spiritual sisters as well as children of the same parents.

Theresa could not only pray that something wonderful would happen to open the way to Carmel. She had to take a step. That step was to ask Papa's permission. She chose the feast of Pentecost, May 29, 1887. The Martins attended afternoon vespers. When they came home Papa went out to the garden and was sitting near the well enjoying the flowers. His hands were folded as if he were praying. Theresa silently sat down next to him. She had so much to say but couldn't find the words.

Papa looked at his youngest daughter and saw tears welling in her eyes. He hugged her close to his heart. He asked her why she was crying. Then he raised her to a standing position, and still holding her close, he walked slowly with her in the garden.

"I want to enter Carmel, too, Papa," she said, relieved that the words were finally out. The tears continued to fall. Papa accepted the choice of his little queen. His tears joined with hers. He was so understanding that Theresa talked on and on about the work of Jesus in her soul. Then Theresa's father went over to the garden wall and plucked a flower. He explained how God had created that beautiful flower, made it grow, cared for it and loved it. Theresa understood that the flower's story was her story. God had placed her in this loving family with parents and sisters who cherished her. Now the flower would leave the family garden and Papa's loving protection. But the Heavenly Father would wait for Theresa at Carmel.

Papa was a deeply spiritual man. He recognized that the moment had come to let his little queen follow her vocation. Theresa placed the flower, roots and all, in her book, *The Imitation of Christ*. She laid it carefully on the first page of the chapter entitled "One Must Love Jesus above All Things."

Trials Before the Dream Comes True

Theresa was jubilant. Papa had given his permission and his blessing for her to follow her dream of joining Carmel. The next step was to ask Uncle Guerin for his permission as well since he was her guardian. Theresa stood before her uncle. It was so different from approaching Papa. Uncle was gentle and kind. But his words were the opposite of what Theresa wanted to hear. Uncle Guerin said *no*. He did not want to talk about the subject again until Theresa was seventeen.

Theresa was speechless. Two weeks passed. Even when she was in the Guerin home, her uncle never mentioned her vocation. She was bursting to ask him again, but she didn't dare. On Saturday, October 22, Theresa went to the Guerins. Before she could even ask to see her uncle, he called her into his study.

Uncle Guerin had a good heart. He had struggled with the way he had responded to Theresa a few weeks before. Along with his good heart, he was a man of prayer. He asked the Lord to help him have a change of heart if this was what God wanted. He received what he had asked for. He told Theresa that he no longer had any problem with her becoming a sister. He called

her a little flower God wanted for himself. Aunt Guerin also gave her consent.

But the road was not yet clear. The priest who had the responsibility of accepting candidates at the Lisieux Carmel told Theresa that she could not enter until she was twenty-one. He was cold and formal. Of course, he added, if the bishop wanted to make an exception, he could. Papa willingly took Theresa to see Bishop Hugonin on October 31, 1887. The bishop was like a father to Theresa. He was impressed by Mr. Martin's approval of his daughter's entrance into Carmel at such a young age. He was equally impressed by the generosity of the young woman. But he did not give a definite answer. He said only that he would have to think the matter over before making a decision. Theresa cried. Bishop Hugonin put his arm around her and consoled her. Papa looked on silently, hoping that his little queen would be able to bear this further delay without too much pain.

The bishop rose and Mr. Martin knew that their meeting was over. Bishop Hugonin told Theresa that she would receive a letter from him while she was in Italy. He blessed them and

Father Reverony, his secretary, walked them to the door. Papa turned to the priest. He reminded Father Reverony of the pilgrimage he and the Martins would be making to Rome. Theresa might have the opportunity to take her request in person to the pope.

The Pilgrimage

Three days after Theresa's interview with the bishop, Papa, Theresa and Celine joined the group of pilgrims from their diocese, Bayeux, and the neighboring diocese, Coutances, on a pilgrimage. It had been organized to celebrate Pope Leo XIII's fifty years of priesthood. Bishop Germain of Coutances would lead the pilgrimage. The Martins were thrilled to be part of such a joyful celebration. And to think they would even meet His Holiness, Pope Leo XIII. Papa, Theresa and Celine thought of their journey as an opportunity for prayer and spiritual growth. They would see Rome with their own eyes and experience that city of martyrs. There the faith of millions, witnessed by their martyrdom, had blessed the Church. The pilgrimage of the French travelers led to Paris, France; Switzerland; and various cities of Italy—Milan, Venice, Bologna, Loreto, Rome, Naples, Pompeii, Assisi, Florence, Pisa and Genoa.

***

On Friday, November 4, the Martins boarded a train that took them to Paris, the capital of their country. Papa enjoyed the train ride. As the train moved down the track, the whistle blew and smoke came from the stacks. Papa sang to the rhythm of the motion: "Roll, roll, my carriage, here we are on the open road." They arrived in the train station and gazed at the city. It looked so inviting. They had three days to sightsee before joining the pilgrimage. Excitement mounted in Celine and Theresa. Before the trip, both girls had been very sad that Theresa's request to enter Carmel had been denied by the bishop. Celine hoped that Pope Leo would grant her sister's request. Theresa felt her only hope rested in Pope Leo XIII. She was anxious to go to Rome on the one hand, and afraid on the other. So much depended on that one meeting with the pope. But for now, she wanted to enjoy Paris, especially the shrine of her Heavenly Mother, Our Lady of Victories. She poured out her soul to the Mother of God in front of the beautiful statue.

The Martins joined the pilgrimage on Monday, November 7. They felt at home with their fellow pilgrims. Although many of the lay people were wealthy, they were friendly and interesting. Bishop Germain of Coutances led the pilgrimage. Many priests were in the group, among them Father Reverony, their own bishop's secretary. He had witnessed the touching scene when Theresa had begged Bishop Hugonin to enter Carmel. The priest had been confused by her generous decision to follow her call. He was equally baffled by the generosity of the distinguished old gentleman who was her father. But was this call genuine? The priest smiled to himself. It couldn't be. Anyway, Theresa could be given the permission still, from the pope. But was it likely?

Milan, Venice, Padua, Bologna and Loreto

The first city the pilgrims visited was Milan. They went to the cathedral and examined the gleaming white marble building. Theresa noted in her *Story of a Soul* that the statues "were so many they could have formed a small population." Theresa and Celine were adventurous, eager to see and hear everything. They wanted every opportunity to grasp the religious experience this pilgrimage offered. They decided to stay as close to Bishop Germain as possible. They were like his respectful body guards, remaining alert while the guides talked about the relics of saints and other important visitor information.

Bishop Germain celebrated Mass at the tomb of St. Charles Borromeo, one of the great bishops of Milan. Theresa and Celine joined Papa behind the altar. They wanted to be as close as possible to the tomb of such a great saint. The girls rested their heads familiarly on it as if listening for some secret message from the well-known saint.

After Mass, most of the pilgrims climbed the steps into the spires that shot up in the air like needle points. Higher and higher they trudged up the steps until they arrived at the inside of the bell tower. They looked down. The city of Milan stretched out like a carpet. People seemed as small as insects. Theresa gazed in silence. The wonder of it could take a person's breath away.

The pilgrims went on tours in horse-drawn carriages. They also visited the famous *Campo Santo* cemetery. The respect and love the people of Milan showed deceased family members was impressive. Magnificently chiseled marble statues seemed to keep silent vigil while visitors came to pray. A constant stream of quiet people paid their respects to those who had gone to the next life. Theresa, who had lost her own mother so young, found her belief in a human being's immortal soul a wonderful gift of the mercy of Jesus.

The pilgrims' next stop was Venice, which looked completely different from Milan. The streets were waterways where boatsmen called gondoliers rode up and down with their passengers. The French tourists were fascinated and enjoyed the sights. They traveled on to the city made famous by the Franciscan, St. Anthony—Padua. There the pilgrims venerated a precious relic of the saint.

The pilgrims went next to Bologna, the city of St. Catherine of Bologna. The

city was crowded with students at that time of year. Some were quite unruly. One of them shouted, "Look at the beautiful blonde," and flinging his arms around Theresa, tossed her in the air. She broke free and fixed him with a stare that wiped the smile off his face. Theresa knew how to defend herself and would stand for no nonsense. Theresa and Celine soon forgot the annoyance when they arrived at Loreto, Italy. They went to see the lovely house that the Holy Family lived in at Nazareth. The holy house, it is said, was carried miraculously to its present location. People from all over the world still go to pray in that beautiful place of peace and love. Theresa of the Child Jesus is one of many saints who have found their way there.

Theresa and Celine were especially happy to receive Jesus in Holy Communion during Mass in the house of Loreto. The house was inside a magnificent basilica built by faithful and loving Christians. Theresa spoke to Jesus in those peaceful surroundings. She wanted to join Carmel at the age of fifteen, if the pope would give permission. Surely Jesus would listen to her plea coming to him from that house so familiar to him as a child. Here he had once sat on Mary's lap and rested his head on Joseph's strong shoulder. "Jesus," she prayed, "I know that you love me. Let me be your bride."

Rome—the Coliseum

The French pilgrims arrived in Rome during the night of November 13, 1887. Theresa rose to the porter's calls of "Rome, Rome!" She was really there. Theresa glanced up at the fancy architecture of the buildings. There was something special about the city. Clues of the impact of the Church on the culture of the people were everywhere. The Coliseum, in early Christian times, had been the public arena. Thousands of Romans had crowded to see games of competition. When the persecution of the Church began during the reign of Emperor Nero, Christians were murdered for sport. It was in this very Coliseum that worshipers of Jesus were crucified, fed to wild animals and killed in the cruelest ways. The pagan crowds had considered these public slaughters entertainment. The French pilgrims of Theresa's time were moved by the thought of the Roman martyrs whose blood had given growth to the infant Church.

When Theresa and Celine stood with Papa and gazed into the large, empty stone ruins, they were silent. The walls were crumbling and ropes blocked the entrance to visitors while workmen made their repairs. Theresa wanted to climb down the incline and enter the arena. Celine agreed. While the pilgrims listened to guides explaining the sculptured designs on marble columns, the girls slipped through the barricade and down onto the flat surface of the arena. Papa saw them. He was surprised and tried to wave them back, but they did not seem to notice. So Mr. Martin remained calm, blending in with the group. He knew he would have done what his daughters were doing if he were thirty years younger.

Theresa and Celine searched for a flat piece of pavement marked with a cross. On this spot, men, women and children had given their lives for Jesus. The girls found it and knelt in the dust, praising the Lord for the example of those Christian heroes. While Theresa was kneeling there, she asked Jesus for the grace to be a martyr. She felt in her soul that her prayer was granted. The two young women climbed cautiously back up the incline and slipped into the group. Papa smiled. They showed him the small stones they had gathered near the most sacred spot in the Coliseum.

From there the pilgrims went to the catacombs, underground tunnels that had been dug and used by the early Christian community fleeing government persecution.

The pilgrims spent six days touring Rome. The seventh day was the most exciting of all: the group from France would have an audience with Pope Leo XIII.

A Daring Plan

Theresa had received a letter from Mother Agnes—her sister Pauline—explaining that Bishop Hugonin would not let her enter Carmel at age fifteen. Theresa had hoped to receive a letter from the bishop granting the permission, but no letter had come from him at all. Tension mounted as she realized that the one person who could still grant her request was the pope. Her religious vocation now hinged entirely on her meeting with him. Papa was not aware of the struggle and anxiety Theresa faced. Celine alone shared the tension and the *great plan*.

The pilgrims went for Mass in the pope's chapel on Sunday, November 20, at 8 AM. After Mass, the pope knelt in silent thanksgiving while the pilgrims knelt in silence too. Theresa stared at the praying pontiff. There he was—the one person who could sail her little boat right into Carmel. Would he? The excitement mounted.

The group was told that the Holy Father would greet each pilgrim personally. The women formed in line; then the men. The pilgrims would kneel before the pope, kiss his hand and receive his blessing. To save time, they were asked not to start conversations with His Holiness because of his failing health. Theresa could not believe that last minute instruction. To make matters worse, Father Reverony, her own bishop's secretary, was standing securely next to the pope's chair. Theresa turned anxiously to Celine for advice. What should she do when it was her turn to kneel before the pope? "Speak," Celine whispered. And *speak* Theresa did!

Theresa was kneeling before him. "Holy Father, I have a favor to ask you." The pope leaned toward her to hear her small voice. Father Reverony looked confused and alert. A Swiss guard stood on either side of the girl. "Holy Father, in honor of your Jubilee, permit me to enter Carmel at fifteen!" There, she had said it, exactly as she had rehearsed it, over and over. The pope turned to Father Reverony, probably for more explanation. The priest explained that Theresa was a child who desired to enter Carmel at fifteen, but the superiors were still considering her request.

"Well, my child," the pope said simply, "do what the superiors tell you." Theresa rested her folded hands on the pope's knees and begged, "Oh, Holy Father, if you say yes, everybody will agree!"

Pope Leo XIII said slowly, kindly, "Go . . . go . . . . You will enter if God wills it!" That was true, no one could deny it. But what Theresa really wanted was one sentence that gave her permission to enter the Carmelite Order at fifteen. She tried to continue the conversation. But two Swiss guards tapped her on the shoulders, indicating it was time to move on. Since she did not move, they helped her to her feet. She was still trying to speak as the pope reached out his hand and touched her lips. Then he blessed her.

Tears flowed down her cheeks as the Swiss guards carried her forcibly to the door.

Papa's meeting with the pope had been very consoling. After the audience, he met his two girls and was distressed to see his little queen in tears. As time went on, Theresa realized that the Holy Father's final answer was the only right answer. She would join Carmel if it was the will of God. It couldn't be any other way. But for now, the obstacles seemed so great and the goal so far away.

The pilgrims continued on their way to Naples, Pompeii, Assisi and Florence. They made a return visit to Pisa and Genoa, then went back into France. They arrived at Lisieux during the afternoon of December 2.

The Longest "Wait"

Theresa visited Carmel right away. She had a warm reunion with Pauline after nearly a month. So much had happened in that time. Theresa was still hoping to enter the convent on Christmas. She had taken her request to the pope. That was as far as it could go. The rest was up to God. What was the next move? Pauline suggested that Theresa write a letter to Bishop Hugonin. Theresa did write one and showed it to her uncle to check wording and approach. He was not satisfied and rewrote it. Just when they were about to mail it, Pauline notified

Theresa and told her to wait. She held on to her letter until she received word from her sister. Ten days before Christmas, Theresa was finally told to mail the letter.

Theresa imagined that the bishop would send an instant reply. She and Papa went to the post office every morning after Mass. The letter didn't come. Christmas drew closer. No answer. Christmas arrived and Theresa was still waiting to follow her call to Carmel. During midnight Mass, Theresa began to realize that Jesus was with her, as much as he had been with her on the previous Christmas. That was when he had changed her heart, had given her the grace to grow up. Now he was giving her the opportunity to deepen her trust in him. He seemed to be asleep in her little boat, and she realized that she would please him very much if she would not wake him up.

Christmas afternoon Theresa paid a visit to Carmel. Suddenly the day was transformed as the grill opened. The nuns were there, holding a statue of the Baby. They had placed a ball in his hand. Theresa's name was printed on it. This made her so happy. She was like a toy, a little ball that Jesus could play with or toss into a corner whenever he wanted to. The Carmelites sang a song Pauline had written for Theresa. What a wonderful surprise!

On New Year's Day, 1888, Theresa received a letter. It was from Mother Marie Gonzague, superior of the Carmel of Lisieux. She explained that on December 28, 1887, Bishop Hugonin had granted his permission for Theresa to enter Carmel. However, she would have to wait until Lent was over. The Lenten penances of Carmel would be too hard for someone so young.

This meant that Theresa had arrived at the final delay—three more months—in her journey to Carmel.

Farewell to the House that Was Home

April 9, 1888, was special for two reasons. First, the feast of the Annunciation had been moved from March 25 because of Lent. Second, this day had been chosen as the day on which Theresa would enter Carmel. The evening before, the Martins and Guerins gathered for supper in the Martin home. It was a time of both joy and pain. Papa had grown used to bringing his daughters to the convent door, but Theresa was the youngest. She would always be his little queen.

Papa was quiet but others filled the gap. Uncle Guerin showered his niece with compliments. Marie Guerin called Theresa aside and whispered apologies for whatever she may have done or said to hurt her cousin. Mrs. Guerin sniffed and dabbed her eyes now and then. Leonie, who had left the Visitation Order on January 6, kissed and hugged her youngest sister. After everything was over, Celine and Theresa spent the night talking. They shared their memories and hopes.

In the morning, the Martins rose early and dressed for church. They would be meeting the Guerins at Mass, so the family could participate in the Eucharist and receive Communion with Theresa. The little queen walked

outside and looped her arm through Papa's, the way she always did. Together Theresa and the king walked down the street along with Leonie and Celine.

Theresa pulled on Papa's arm and whispered something. They stopped and she turned to gaze at the house she loved so much. Papa waited patiently, his heart ready to burst. What would he be coming back to? His little queen would not be there to kiss his forehead and walk with him arm in arm. Papa's gift to the King of kings was cheerfully, though painfully, given. After Mass, Theresa hugged and kissed each relative. Then, with her arm in Papa's, she walked to the front door of Carmel.

This was the great moment. At times it had seemed to Theresa to be the impossible moment. Now it was really true. She felt her heart beating rapidly as they approached the convent door. Theresa knelt down and asked her father for his blessing. The humble old man did something she never expected. He, too, knelt on the ground, then blessed his child. Tears streamed down his cheeks. Theresa hugged her king as the doors of the convent opened wide. She went in and the gates closed. Her own sisters,

Pauline and Marie, were there to greet her. Mother Marie Gonzague, the prioress, welcomed her.

Theresa was only fifteen years old, but she became deeply convinced that Carmel was where she belonged. Here she would find *peace*. "I'm here forever!"

Life at Carmel

Theresa was a postulant—a person preparing to become a religious. Everything was new and different from the daily life she had known. The convent surroundings were plain, almost bare, in contrast to the beautiful furnishings she once had. Her heart opened to a quiet, soothing peace. The schedule was strict but balanced. Her day included prayer, rest, work, recreation and free time. The center of her life was Jesus. The center of her day was private prayer, meditation and, of course, the Eucharistic Celebration.

The Carmel of Lisieux had about twenty nuns. They were all ages, but Postulant Theresa, at fifteen, was the youngest. She was especially impressed by Mother Genevieve of St. Teresa. In 1838 Mother Genevieve had come from the Carmel of Poitiers, France, to begin the Carmel of Lisieux. She was eighty-three years old when she came into Theresa's life. She knelt silent and motionless in the convent chapel. Her dark eyes were riveted to the Blessed Sacrament. What was she saying to her Spouse? How did he respond? Only Jesus and the holy old Carmelite nun knew. Just to see Mother Genevieve was thrilling. Theresa never forgot her.

Theresa also admired Mother Marie Gonzague, the prioress. Mother had been kind and gentle with her before she came to Carmel, but now she seemed distant and stern. Theresa was puzzled by Mother's changed attitude. Mother Gonzague was being very careful not to spoil Theresa. She certainly was not the little queen there. Theresa had understood that religious life would be a challenge. It was hard, but she realized that her effort to accept the constant little sacrifices every day would be the way she would carry her cross with Jesus. She knew that the joy and peace of Carmel had a price, the way the stem of a beautiful rose has thorns. But knowing what to expect did not make the thorns easier to bear.

Theresa prayed, joined happily in the times of community recreation and learned the ways of her new life. She also folded laundry and kept the linen closet in order.

She was overjoyed when her oldest sister, Marie, professed her vows six weeks after her own entrance to Carmel. Marie's profession was on May 22, 1888. She was called Sister Marie of the Sacred Heart. Father Pichon, Theresa's spiritual director, came for her sister's profession. The kindly priest helped Theresa grow in the spiritual life. But on November 3 of that year, Father Pichon was transferred to Canada. Theresa's contact with this helpful spiritual guide would now be only through letters.

Theresa received frightening news: On Saturday, June 23, 1888, Papa had disappeared. He had suffered a mild stroke a year before, but had recovered. Now his frantic daughters, Celine and Leonie joined Uncle Guerin to search for him. They found Mr. Martin on June 27 in La Havre. He had suffered a second attack. His daughters at Carmel had worried and prayed for his safe return. Papa's health gradually improved enough for him to come to Carmel on January 10, 1889. That was the date Bishop Hugonin had set for Theresa to receive her religious habit. The bishop himself would perform the ceremony.

Theresa, in her bridal gown and veil, came out of the cloister into the entranceway where Papa waited. He hugged her and whispered, *"My little queen, my little queen."*

Then the bride of Jesus looped her arm through the arm of her king. Together they walked down the aisle to the front of the chapel. Uncle Guerin was there too. He kept his head slightly bowed to hide his tears.

The ceremony was beautiful, and Papa enjoyed it most of all. He would hold back nothing from Jesus, not even his pearl, his little queen. The ceremony ended with the singing of a special hymn of praise to God that was usually sung only during profession ceremonies. The bishop himself made the exception that day and led the community in the singing of the *Te Deum.*

After the ceremony, Theresa and Papa walked up the aisle and through the door. They hugged each other while tears of joy lit their eyes. Papa now knew that Celine would eventually follow her call to Carmel. And on June 24, 1893, Leonie would enter again the convent of the Visitation only to leave on July 20, 1895. In 1899, two years after Theresa's death, Leonie re-entered the Visitation convent and stayed. Papa's five girls would all be brides of Jesus. Nothing could have made him happier.

Theresa kissed Papa, who then left the cloister and stepped into the brisk afternoon air. After he was gone, she looked through the window and realized that snow had fallen. The ground was covered with a soft, white blanket. "Have I ever told you how much I love snow?" Theresa wrote. "When I was small, its whiteness filled me with delight, and one of the greatest pleasures I had was taking a walk under the light snow flakes."

Papa left shoe marks in the freshly fallen snow as he made his way back home. Inside the grill, Bishop Hugonin hugged Sister Theresa gently. He talked about the appointment Papa and Theresa had with him when she was just fourteen years old. He described her hair piled on top of her head so that she would look older. Theresa just smiled as the bishop kept saying proudly that she was his little girl. She thought of Papa, nearly home by now. Too bad he could not hear the bishop's conversation. But then, Jesus heard it all, and he would know how to tell her king.

Papa's Crown

Theresa realized on her wedding day that Papa's illness caused him much suffering. Whatever Papa had to bear was painful for her and the family as well. Little by little, Theresa deepened her awareness of the value of the cross in her life. First it would mean to recognize what shape and

form her cross would take. Then it would mean lifting it up to Jesus with love. Papa's illness was the most recent cross, but there had been others: the death of her mother, her difficult years at the boarding school, her mysterious illness, Pauline's and Marie's departures from home, her own time of waiting to enter Carmel. Yes, Theresa's sensitive heart had felt the thorns keenly. She had learned to go to Jesus for answers. She was a good listener, and waited in silent expectation for the voice of her Spouse.

On February 12 Papa's condition had become so bad that he had to be admitted to the Catholic hospital for the mentally ill in Caen. Celine and Leonie boarded at the orphanage of St. Vincent de Paul to be near their father. They were his loving supports during this long ordeal. His daughters at Carmel were united, too, in their daily prayers and dedication to their duties. Pauline, Marie and Theresa took Papa's welfare to heart. They, too, walked his Calvary. They were in the company of their crucified Jesus.

Theresa the Novice

Theresa had now entered the noviatiate. She considered Jesus her novice master. There was so much to learn from her Spouse. She had a novice mistress, too, a Carmelite nun named Sister Marie of the Angels. The novice mistress was gentle and kind. But Mother Gonzague, the prioress, continued to be stern with Theresa. Even though Theresa was young, the prioress wanted to challenge her to mature in the spiritual life. She loved Theresa although her words and actions were not always loving. Theresa swept the hallways. In the dim sunlight, it was easy to miss a cobweb. But if Theresa missed it, Mother Gonzague did not. She said out loud in front of everyone, "We can easily see that the cloisters are swept by a child of fifteen." Theresa winced. She felt like crying. Once she had tasted criticism and rejection at the boarding school, and had taken those hurts to Jesus. He had soothed her heart and helped her give over those sufferings to him. Then her loving Savior united them with his passion and death, the perfect sacrifice to the Heavenly Father. Theresa asked Jesus to help her now to offer up the scolding with love and to do her tasks more diligently.

Sometimes the other nuns wanted to sympathize with Theresa. They realized that Mother Gonzague was challenging her out of love. After all, Theresa had come from a loving family and had been the youngest child. But Theresa did not need sympathy. She quietly accepted the challenge. She was open to letting God work in her heart. She must have wished that Mother Gonzague would change her ways. But as time went on, Theresa began to understand why she didn't. If Mother Gonzague had been kind and gentle, Theresa could have given her all her attention and affection. Mother Gonzague could have replaced Papa and her sisters. But that was not why she had come to Carmel, she realized. She had come to fill her heart with Jesus, to give herself totally to him. So Theresa put all her effort into living the religious life. She would do this by offering up countless little daily sacrifices to her Spouse.

The convent of Lisieux did not have electricity. Each nun's room was lit by a small oil lamp. Oil had to be added daily. Theresa went one evening to pick up her lamp to prepare it for the night. Only one lamp remained. It was large and bulky and chipped.

Theresa's small delicate lamp had been taken. At first, she felt resentful that her lamp was not there. Then another thought came: she could offer up that small act of injustice, and quietly use the leftover lamp. She would do this as an act of love for Jesus. Theresa's face remained serene as she walked away with her lamp to the quiet of her room.

***

One time, the novice mistress found a small vase broken on the window sill near Theresa's room. She assumed that Theresa had broken it accidentally, but had forgotten to mention it. Theresa had not broken it. She had not even seen that it was broken. The novice mistress, in her soft-spoken way, said to Theresa, "Be more careful next time." Theresa thanked her and promised to be more careful in the future. The little incident showed Theresa how human it is to feel injustice. She, too, cared very much about her reputation. It was only right that she declare her innocence. She did not have to take the blame for something she didn't do. On the other hand, no harm was going to come to her or anybody else if she accepted this false accusation in humility. In this way, she could show her love for Jesus. That is what she did.

Theresa learned to look into her heart and talk to Jesus. She offered her prayers, her sufferings, her daily household tasks. She swept and scrubbed the hallways. She took care of the dining room—filling the water pitchers, cleaning the tables, sweeping and scrubbing the floor, keeping the cupboards in order. She asked the Lord for strength to live with gratitude her beautiful calling.

The Great Day of Religious Profession

Theresa had learned about and lived the life of Carmel as a postulant and as a novice. Now she was asking permission to give her life to Jesus by making vows of poverty, chastity and obedience. Through the *vow of poverty* she would promise to be satisfied with what was given her and to be self-sacrificing. She would not be able to own things, the way she would have if she had remained a lay person. Through the *vow of chastity*, she would freely give her love, her energies, her body and soul to Jesus. She would work and pray for his people, the Church. Through the *vow of obedience* she would promise her will to Jesus. She would obey her superiors and respect them as representatives of God.

Theresa professed her vows on September 8, the feast of the birthday of Mary. All during the night before, her sleep was restless and broken. She was tempted by the devil, who wanted her to believe that she really was not called to be a nun. He let her fear that she would never remain faithful to her vows, never remain in her vocation until death. Maybe she should not go ahead with it. Perhaps in the morning, she could go to the prioress and ask her to notify the bishop. She could

never make it, never . . . . Theresa called out, half awake, half asleep, "Jesus, help me. Jesus, don't leave me. Jesus, don't let me leave you."

In the morning, when she awoke, the terrible doubt was gone. In its place was peace. Theresa pronounced her vows, joyfully. Over her heart she carried a handwritten letter to her Spouse. This letter contains the key to the rest of her short life:

"O Jesus, my Divine Spouse!
May I never lose the second robe of my baptism.
Take me before I can commit the slightest voluntary fault.
May I never seek nor find anything but Yourself alone.
May creatures be nothing for me, and may I be nothing for them,
but may you, Jesus, be everything!
May the things of earth never be able to trouble my soul,
and may nothing disturb my peace.
Jesus, I ask you for nothing but peace, and also love,
infinite love without any limits other than yourself;
love which is no longer I but you, my Jesus.
Jesus, may I die a martyr for you.
Give me martyrdom of heart or of body, or rather give me both.
Give me grace to fulfill my vows in all their perfection,
and make me understand what a real spouse should be.
Never let me be a burden to the community,
let nobody be occupied with me,
let me be looked upon as trampled underfoot,
forgotten like your little grain of sand, Jesus.
May your will be done in me perfectly,
and may I arrive at the place you have prepared for me.
Jesus, allow me to save very many souls;
let no soul be lost today;
let all the souls in purgatory be saved.
Jesus, pardon me if I say anything I should not say.
I want only to give you joy and to console you."

Sister Theresa of the Child Jesus
(From *Story of A Soul,* Institute of Carmelite Studies)

Joy and Sorrow
—Heavenly Gifts

On September 24 Theresa received the veil of Carmel. Theresa's religious name was Sister Theresa of the Child Jesus. Although she could not know that day, she had only seven more years to live. Those seven years were to leave a glorious witness that would spread rapidly throughout the world after her death. Her years at Carmel would provide the atmosphere for Theresa to deepen her living of the way of what she called *spiritual childhood*. Like the little children of the gospels, who crowded around Jesus without fear and with such openness of heart, so would little Theresa. She was a spiritual child, not childish but childlike. She was willing to risk being considered a child for Jesus' sake. After all, he welcomed little children and blessed them (cf. Mt. 19:13-15). The children of the gospels loved and trusted Jesus. They had no fear of him, only *trust*. That is what Theresa aimed for in her own life: she wanted to abandon her whole life to Jesus' will. She wanted him to guide the sails of her tiny boat into the sea whenever and wherever he wanted. This was easier to say than to live, as Theresa's years at Carmel will show. Theresa's devotion to the Child Jesus was so important to

her that she chose to include that name in her own.

The other part of Theresa's name, the *Holy Face*, helped her grow in love for Jesus as her Redeemer. She would dedicate her life to making up for all that Jesus suffered after he was condemned to death. She would love and console the beaten, disfigured Jesus, whose sacred head had been crowned with thorns. Theresa would be there in his suffering and agony. She believed, too, that some day, in heaven, she would share in his glory.

***

Papa's health continued to fail. The strokes caused partial paralysis. Celine had hoped that she could bring her father to Carmel for at least the last part of the ceremony when Theresa received the veil. It would have meant so much to both Theresa and her father if Papa could have given his blessing on that occasion. Mr. Martin's absence brought pain to his sensitive daughter. Now she would bring her tears to the Lord to accept for the salvation of his people. Mr. Martin was well enough to visit Carmel on May 12, 1892. That was his last visit. Marie, Pauline and

Theresa talked with him through the grill. The holy man died on July 29, 1894. He was seventy years old.

Theresa lived with Mother Genevieve, the foundress of the Lisieux Carmel. In fact, Theresa was one of the nuns who kept vigil in turn at her bedside when she was dying. In her last agony, one tear appeared on the rim of her eyelid and stayed there, gleaming. Theresa noticed that it remained even after Mother Genevieve was dead. The young nun took a small piece of linen cloth and touched it to the eyelid. The tear moistened the cloth. Sister Theresa looked at it reverently and treasured her relic. She wrote in her *Story of a Soul* that she believed Mother Genevieve was a saint. The nun died on December 5, 1891, at the age of eighty-six. A few nights later, Theresa had a beautiful dream. Mother Genevieve had the nuns gathered around her. She was writing her will. As she did, she left something precious for each of her dear sisters. Because Theresa was the youngest, she seemed to wait a long time. She started to think that there would be nothing left for her. But when her turn came, Mother Genevieve said, "To you I give my heart." Mother said this three times very distinctly. Then the dream was over.

***

A month later, the flu swept through the community. Only three nuns remained well enough to care for the others. Theresa was one of them. Death, too, entered the young nun's life once again. Three nuns died in the span of a few days. Sister St. Joseph, the oldest member of the community, died on January 2, 1892, Theresa's nineteenth birthday. Theresa found Sister Magdalene in her room, sleeping peacefully in death, and Sister Febronie died on January 4. Since the sister sacristan was very ill, Theresa prepared the chapel for the funeral liturgies. She was overwhelmed, yet each of the sisters had lived long, full religious lives. Imagine their joy in heavenly glory. Theresa exclaimed, "All through the time the community was undergoing this trial, I had the unspeakable consolation of receiving Holy Communion *every day*!"

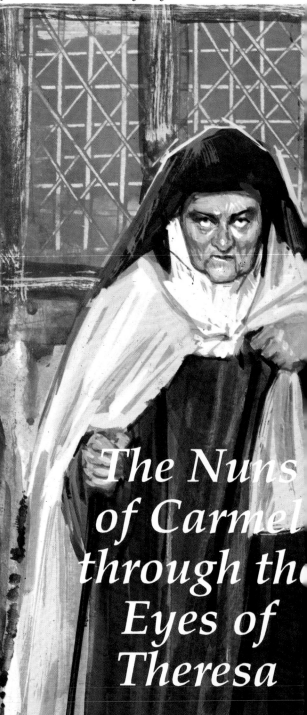

The Nuns of Carmel through the Eyes of Theresa

The elderly Sister St. Pierre was one of the nuns whom Sister Theresa became a real sister to. Their friendship had been one-sided at first as the younger nun, still a novice, reached out lovingly to be of service. Theresa knelt in chapel directly in front of Sister St. Pierre at evening prayer. Theresa noticed that at ten minutes to six it was time for some kindly member to begin to help the elderly sister make the journey to the dining room. The old nun lived in constant pain caused by arthritis. She did not like to have new helpers, but relied on those she felt secure with. Theresa offered to take her to the dining room. Her offer was received cautiously at first. There was a definite routine involved. There was an exact time, the right pace, the same chair in the proper place. Theresa mastered the routine. She went out of her way to take care of the details. She wrote, "Each evening when I saw Sister St. Pierre shake her hour-glass I knew this meant: Let's go!"

Theresa would immediately stand, take Sister St. Pierre's small bench and put it in the exact spot reserved for it. Then she would put her arm through the elderly nun's arm and slowly, carefully walk with her to the dining room. She always let Sister St. Pierre set the pace. She never hurried her. Sometimes Sister complained that Theresa was too fast or too slow. She was going to fall. But she didn't.

After a few days, Sister Theresa noticed that as the meal began, Sister St. Pierre had a difficult time cutting her bread. Her crippled hands could not grasp the knife securely. Theresa asked if she could cut the bread for her. She let the nun show her how she wanted it. Then Theresa added this to the ritual. Night after night, Theresa was there for her. And slowly, the stern look on the old nun's face, caused by years of pain, melted. The pain was still there, but it didn't hurt so much now. She saw in the gentle face of Theresa a love that was like the love of Jesus for her.

Sister St. Pierre

79

Celine Comes to Carmel

On February 20, 1893, Pauline—Sister Agnes of Jesus—was elected prioress. She was to serve for one term of three years. Mother Gonzague was appointed novice mistress. Sister Theresa of the Child Jesus was her assistant. On January 2, 1894, Theresa turned twenty-one. On January 21 she and the novices performed the play she had written: *Joan of Arc*. Theresa had the leading role.

***

Theresa waited and prayed for her sister, Celine, to enter Carmel. Celine had been so devoted to Papa during his final, painful years. Theresa would never forget her dear king's last visit to Carmel. He was so frail, a shade of his former self. Celine and Uncle Guerin helped him along, knowing just what to do. Papa had slowly lifted his eyes upward, gazing at something he alone saw. Then he formed a word carefully on his lips: "Heaven, heaven." Papa died on July 29, 1894.

One of the nuns, Sister Aimee of Jesus, opposed Celine's entrance into Carmel. She gave as her reason that three sisters from the same family was sufficient. The nun was firmly convinced that she was right. A reverse decision seemed humanly impossible. Theresa was hurt. She also wanted the peace of knowing that Papa had gone straight to heaven. After his long time of suffering, she could not believe anything else for him. She took her worry to her Spouse and asked for a sign. If Sister Aimee of Jesus would change her mind about Celine, she would know that Papa had gone straight to heaven. As Theresa left chapel, a nun slowly approached her. It was Sister Aimee. She smiled and asked Theresa if she could speak with her. The two nuns were alone. Tears lit Sister Aimee's eyes as she struggled for words. "I have changed my mind," she said simply.

On September 14, 1894, Celine entered Carmel. Theresa's "other self" was now with her; they were united once again in their love and service of Jesus. Because Theresa was assigned to the novitiate to help Mother Gonzague, Celine was placed under Theresa's guidance. Nearly a year later, on August 15, 1895, their cousin, Marie Guerin, joined them. She would be one of Theresa's novices and would eventually become Sister Marie of the Eucharist.

"My Vocation Is Love"

Children are naturally unafraid. They do not suspect evil or look for it. Theresa had a trusting and affectionate relationship with her family. She had climbed on Papa's lap and placed her head on his chest. She had held his hand securely and skipped along beside him on their walks through the fields and in the park. She had visited churches with Papa and had become aware of the presence of Jesus waiting there in the Blessed Sacrament. When Mama had passed away, Theresa's sisters had lovingly cared for her. They had listened to her, taught her how to do things, answered her questions. The atmosphere of the Martin home was full of peace, not tension. Theresa did not have to risk being misunderstood or rejected. She was trusted and trusting. It was that same kind of love and trust she gave to God.

At Carmel Theresa learned about the greatest of all gifts: *love*. She wanted to put her whole self into the living of her religious life. She wanted to climb the mountain of love. She wrote in her *Story of a Soul*: "Jesus does not demand great actions from us, but simply *surrender* and *gratitude*."

As she read the Bible and *The Imitation of Christ*, her two favorite books,

she searched for her place in Jesus' heart. In the Gospel passages about Jesus' love for children, she found herself. In St. Paul's first letter to the Corinthians, chapter 13, she found the kind of love she could show right there in her own everyday life. St. Paul described love as patient, kind, not jealous, not sophisticated, not boastful or rude, not selfish, nor quick-tempered. Love does not harbor grudges over injuries, does not rejoice over wrongdoing, but rejoices with the truth. Charity puts up with all things, believes all things, hopes all things and doesn't give up. Love never fails.

Theresa meditated on those words until they became a living prayer in her soul. She understood the heart of Paul's message to be in his description of love. This was Christian charity laid out in a clear definition for everyone: for popes, presidents, rich, poor, healthy, sick, educated, uneducated. Theresa in Carmel could live this definition, too. She was hidden and little in the spiritual life. But she made up her mind to love totally and to give her heart to Jesus. She set out to make the gift of her life the best she had to offer. She wanted to hold nothing back. Once, when she was a little child, she

had refused Papa a kiss unless he came to her. She did that just once and never forgot it. Papa did not give much importance to her behavior. After all, his little queen was a child. But the grownup Theresa determined never to tell God "no." She had set her hopes on becoming a saint. She trusted that God would help her accept and follow his will for her. Her trust in him was total and childlike.

Spiritually, Theresa climbed onto the lap of God and learned the secrets of divine love. She began to think about how she wanted to fulfill all the valuable ministries in the Church to please Jesus. She wanted to be a missionary, a priest, a prophet, a preacher, an apostle, even a martyr. Yet how could these desires become real? She was a cloistered nun who never went out of the convent door. She talked to people through a grill and performed ordinary tasks like sweeping the hallway and tidying up the dining room. She spent hours each day in prayer. How could little Theresa be a preacher? A prophet? A missionary? A martyr? She realized that she *could* be all of these because Jesus had set her free. The motive, the power house, the drive behind the Christian had to be love. She would love as much as it was possible for her to love. She wrote joyfully in her *Story of a Soul*, "O Jesus, my Love: my vocation, at last I have found it . . . . My vocation is love!"

Suffering Is a Prayer of Love

At the end of December 1894 Mother Agnes of Jesus (Pauline) asked Theresa to begin to write her childhood memories. Theresa began at once, working on her handwritten remembrances in spare moments. This assignment would become a manuscript called *Story of a Soul.* She wrote the first part, called manuscript A, in 1895. On January 20, 1896, she brought her completed copybook to Mother Agnes.

In the spring of 1894 Theresa began to suffer from throat infections. She received treatments and continued her normal life of prayer and responsibilities to the novices in her care. She wrote poems and plays. She completed a painting in the dining room. On Holy Thursday night, April 2, 1896, Theresa remained, adoring Jesus in the Blessed Sacrament until midnight. She prepared for bed, blew out her lamp, and rested her head on her pillow. She did not realize until that moment how tired she felt. Just then, she coughed. Something warm and bubbling filled her mouth. Could it be blood? The room was too dark to see. She could have gone to find out or get help. But it was so late. Why disturb anyone? Even if it was blood, she did not have to be afraid. It meant that Jesus would be coming for her soon. In the morning, she stared at her blood-stained pillow and she knew she had tuberculosis.

It was Good Friday, April 3, 1896. This was the beginning of Theresa's own walk to Calvary. It would end a year and five months later, on September 30, 1897. That evening she coughed up blood again. On that particular Good Friday, Theresa kept the strict fast and did not ask for any exceptions. She wanted to give her little gift to Jesus, offering up her day for the many people who needed her prayers and sacrifices.

As Theresa's illness spread, she found it almost impossible at times to keep up with the prayers and activities assigned her. But she faithfully did whatever she could. She had the heart of a mother and a missionary. She pushed herself to pray fervently and to make little sacrifices for the spiritual good of the novices entrusted to her guidance. "My dear Mother," she wrote to Pauline, "I am a little brush which Jesus has chosen in order to paint his own image in the souls you entrusted to my care."

On May 10, 1896, Theresa had a dream. She was standing near her own mother. Several other people were in the distance, but she did not know who they were. Just then, she saw three Carmelites enter the room. Theresa understood that these people were in heaven. Only one nun showed her face. She was Venerable Anne of Jesus, who had lived at the time of St. Teresa of Avila in Spain. Mother Anne spoke gently to her. Theresa had the courage to ask her if God would come to take her soon from this earth. "Yes, soon, soon, I promise you," Mother Anne answered. Then, as a child is anxious to win the approval of her parents, Theresa asked, "Is God pleased with me?" Mother Anne looked lovingly on Theresa and answered, "God asks no other thing of you. He is very pleased." Venerable Anne's visit to her in the dream filled Theresa with joy. Sometimes the devil tempted her to doubt the existence of heaven or the truths of the Catholic faith. During those trying times, she remembered that wonderful dream. She trusted with all her heart in Jesus' love for her.

***

On September 8, 1896, Theresa was asked to continue writing her *Story of a Soul.* She wrote manuscript B and addressed it to Jesus. Even though she was very ill, Mother Gonzague asked Theresa to write the final part, manuscript C, of *Story of a Soul.* On July 8 Theresa, now critically ill, was brought to the convent infirmary. Her whole body felt like it was being whipped with the scourges her crucified Jesus had suffered. Breathing became more difficult with each passing day. It seemed as if an invisible pillow was being pressed into her face. The fits of coughing shook her violently and she frequently spit up blood. On July 30 she received the Anointing of the Sick. Theresa was terribly thirsty. Each morning her tongue was as dry as sandpaper—another gift to offer to Jesus for someone most in need.

In her mind, doubts about everything related to faith clung to her and taunted her. She recognized that this trial was a temptation. Jesus would never abandon his little child now. With her imagination, Theresa climbed painfully onto the lap of her Savior and held on to faith. This trial, the most painful of all that she had to suffer, lasted eighteen months. It did end finally, a few moments before her death.

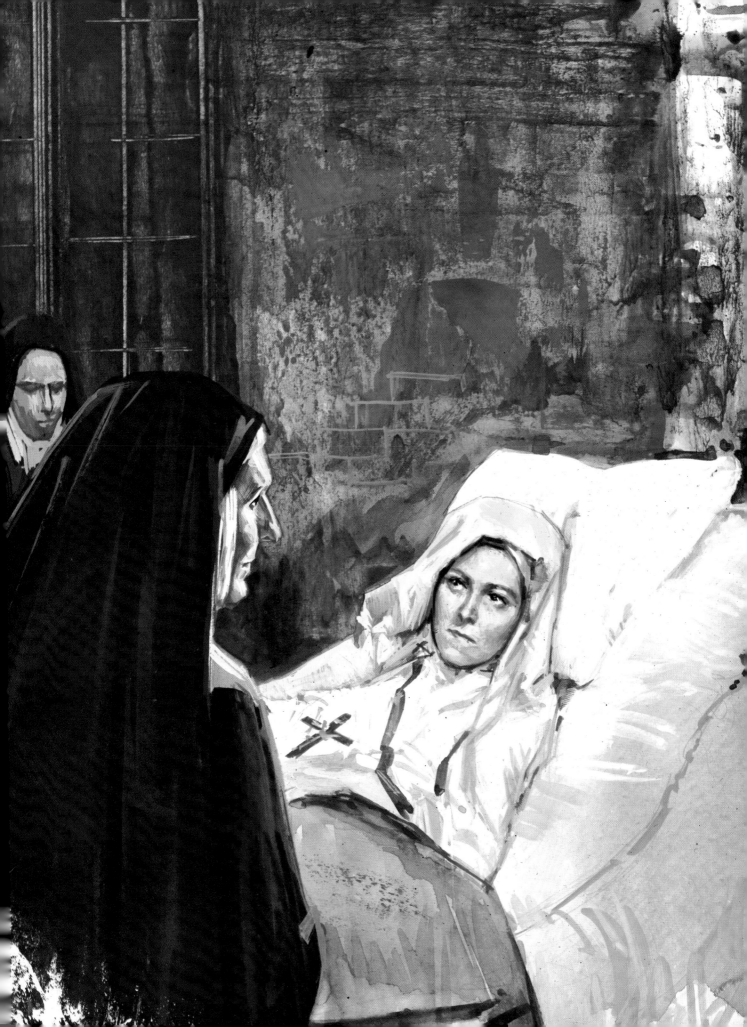

Theresa's Love for the Church

Even when she was dying, Theresa was thinking of others. She asked the nuns to "buy" three mission babies instead of flowers for her funeral. She meant that she wanted to send a donation to help poor children in mission lands. This was the kind of flowers she wanted.

In her way of spiritual childhood, Theresa explained that everything done with love pleases Jesus, no matter how small an action. For example, she said, picking up a pin dropped on the floor by mistake can be pleasing to Jesus. We do it not just to avoid purgatory (punishment for ourselves), but as an act of love.

Another act of love as she lay dying was her peaceful endurance of the flies that buzzed around her in the hot humid summer of 1897.

Theresa had pinned a picture of Theophane Venard on her bed curtains. He was a young French missionary priest born in 1829. He had died a martyr in Hanoi, Indochina (now Hanoi, Vietnam). He was declared "blessed" by Pope Pius X on May 2, 1909, twelve years after the death of Theresa. He was declared a saint by Pope John Paul II in the group of saints called the Martyrs of Vietnam. Father Venard was the missionary whom Theresa wanted to be in her desires, in her prayerfulness and self-sacrifice. She mentioned him often during the final stages of her illness.

The days of September passed slowly. It seemed impossible that a new day could bring Theresa greater suffering than the previous day. But it did. She frequently promised to come down from heaven, to bring graces, a shower of roses, on those who asked her. She promised to come back to help missionaries and to save pagan babies from dying without baptism.

One of the sisters asked Theresa what name should be used to pray to her in heaven. The dying nun smiled and answered quickly, "Call me little Theresa."

Theresa died on Thursday, September 30, 1897. She was buried in the Lisieux cemetery on October 4. And then she was true to her word: she began to send down a shower of roses from heaven. On March 7, 1898, Bishop Hugonin gave his permission for Theresa's *Story of a Soul* to be published.

***

From 1899 to 1902 pilgrims began to come to Theresa's grave to pray. There were reports of favors and cures received. Theresa's cause for sainthood was presented to Rome by the Carmelites on July 9, 1906. In one year, 1910, the Carmel of Lisieux received 9,741 letters from France and beyond. Devotion to Theresa continued to spread. On August 14, 1921 Pope Benedict XV officially began the investigation of Theresa's life. The pope delivered a moving sermon at the ceremony on the importance of her way of spiritual childhood.

On April 29, 1923 Pope Pius XI declared Theresa "blessed." He called her "the star of his pontificate."

On May 17, 1925 the same pope proclaimed Theresa a saint.

Prayers We Can Say to Honor St. Theresa of the Child Jesus

A Prayer to Obtain the Spirit of St. Theresa

O God of Merciful Love, you have never failed your people in any age, but have always raised up saints as lamps to their feet on the road to salvation. We thank you for the waterfall of grace you poured down on St. Theresa of Lisieux. Because she really believed the Gospel she understood it, and you have endowed her with the gift of unfolding its riches for us in our own day. For this we thank you most sincerely, and we ask for the perseverance to follow "the little way" of holiness that you yourself revealed to her.

Teach us to give up our unrealistic dreams of heroism and settle down to the task of being ourselves and accepting what we are. Help us want your will and nothing else—nothing at all, Lord. Help us find it in the real world of every day's here and now. Convince us that the present moment with its light and its darkness, its highs and its lows, its joys and its sorrows, is nothing else than your own dwelling place, your very temple into which you call us to be loved and to love: to love you and to love our brothers and sisters . . . and not least of all to love our own poor wonderful selves.

We ask this through your own dear Son, Our Lord Jesus, who lives and reigns with you in the joyous embrace of the Holy Spirit. One God for always and forever. Amen.

My Novena Rose Prayer

O little Theresa of the Child Jesus,
please pick for me a rose
from the heavenly gardens and
send it to me as a message of love.
O Little Flower of Jesus,
ask God today to grant the favors I now place
with confidence in your hands . . . .
(Mention specific request)
St. Theresa, help me to always believe as you did,
in God's great love for me,
so that I might imitate your "little way" each day.
Amen.

Miraculous Prayer to St. Theresa

O glorious St. Theresa, whom Almighty God has raised up to help and inspire the human family, I beg your miraculous intercession. You are so powerful in obtaining every need of body and spirit from the heart of God. Holy Mother Church proclaims you "prodigy of miracles . . . the greatest saint of modern times." Now I fervently beseech you to answer my petition *(mention here)* and to carry out your promises of *spending heaven doing good upon earth . . . of letting fall from heaven a shower of roses.* Little Flower, give me your childlike faith, to see the face of God in the people and experiences of my life, and to love God with full confidence. St. Theresa of the Child Jesus, I will fulfill your plea "to be made known everywhere" and I will continue to lead others to Jesus through you. Amen.

Novena Prayer
for Vocations

St. Theresa, you answered the Lord's call to become love in the heart of the Church by entering Carmel and living the hidden life of contemplative prayer, fasting, and self-offering for the mission of the Church and the salvation of souls. Through your intercession, hear our prayers for an increase in vocations to the priesthood and religious life in our diocese. Send us laborers for our vineyard who will be true apostles of the Lord, faithful to the service of his truth, the pursuit of holiness, and always sensitive to the needs of others before their own. We ask this through Christ our Lord. Amen.

St. Theresa, patroness of seminarians, pray for us.

Prayer to Learn the "Little Way"
of St. Theresa

Lord Jesus, through the life of St. Theresa with its lesson of trust and simplicity, you have brought new hope to all who long to open their hearts to you in prayer. Teach us the secret of her Little Way and help us to understand that it is not in long prayers of lofty words that we must talk with you. Rather, it is in the deep love with which we bring you our gratitude, our smiles and our tears. Amen.

Stay with Us, Jesus

Stay with us, Jesus, in the midst of our busy hours. When we are tempted, discouraged or burdened in any way, may we with a silent cry of our hearts turn to you in loving trust. Change each passing moment of time into an eternal moment of prayer. And Good Jesus, from your overflowing mercy, fill every troubled human heart with the confident faith of St. Theresa. In joy, in sorrow, in every circumstance, may our hearts rest in your infinite peace. Amen.

Pauline
BOOKS & MEDIA

The Daughters of St. Paul operate book and media centers at the following addresses. Visit, call or write the one nearest you today, or find us on the World Wide Web, www.pauline.org.

CALIFORNIA
3908 Sepulveda Blvd., Culver City, CA 90230   310-397-8676
5945 Balboa Ave., San Diego, CA 92111   619-565-9181
46 Geary Street, San Francisco, CA 94108   415-781-5180
FLORIDA
145 S.W. 107th Ave., Miami, FL 33174   305-559-6715
HAWAII
1143 Bishop Street, Honolulu, HI 96813   808-521-2731
ILLINOIS
172 North Michigan Ave., Chicago, IL 60601   312-346-4228
LOUISIANA
4403 Veterans Memorial Blvd., Metairie, LA 70006   504-887-7631
MASSACHUSETTS
Rte. 1, 885 Providence Hwy., Dedham, MA 02026   781-326-5385
MISSOURI
9804 Watson Rd., St. Louis, MO 63126   314-965-3512
NEW JERSEY
561 U.S. Route 1, Wick Plaza, Edison, NJ 08817   732-572-1200
NEW YORK
150 East 52nd Street, New York, NY 10022   212-754-1110
78 Fort Place, Staten Island, NY 10301   718-447-5071
OHIO
2105 Ontario Street (at Prospect Ave.), Cleveland, OH 44115
   610-621-9427
PENNSYLVANIA
9171-A Roosevelt Blvd., Philadelphia, PA 19114   215-676-9494
SOUTH CAROLINA
243 King Street, Charleston, SC 29401   803-577-0175
TENNESSEE
4811 Poplar Ave., Memphis, TN 38117   901-761-2987
TEXAS
114 Main Plaza, San Antonio, TX 78205   210-224-8101
VIRGINIA
1025 King Street, Alexandria, VA 22314   703-549-3806
CANADA
3022 Dufferin Street, Toronto, Ontario, Canada M6B 3T5
   416-781-9131
1155 Yonge Street, Toronto, Ontario, Canada M4T 1W2;
   416-934-3440

Libros en español!